Kong

The 8th Wonder of the World

Fran Walsh & Philippa Boyens & Peter Jackson

Based on a Story by Merian C. Cooper and Edgar Wallace

Level 2

Retold by Coleen Degnan-Veness
Series Editors: Andy Hopkins and Jocelyn Potter

Pearson Education Limited

Edinburgh Gate, Harlow,
Essex CM20 2JE, England
and Associated Companies throughout the world.

Pack ISBN: 978-1-4058-5208-1
Book ISBN: 978-1-4058-4275-4
CD-ROM ISBN: 978-1-4058-5060-5

This edition first published by Pearson Education Ltd 2007

5 7 9 10 8 6

Set in 12.5/16pt A. Garamond
Printed in China
SWTC/05

Produced for the Publishers by AC Estudio Editorial S.L.

Published by Pearson Education Ltd in association with Penguin Books Ltd,
both companies being subsidiaries of Pearson Plc

Acknowledgements
We are grateful to the following for permission to reproduce photographs:
Getty Images: page 59 (bl) (STF/AFP); **Rex Features:** page 58 (b) (Sipa Press), page 59 (tl) (SNAP),
(tr) (c. Lucasfilm/Everett), (br) (Everett Collection)
All other images and cover image: **Courtesy of Universal Studios Licensing LLLP**
Picture research by Hilary Luckcock

Every effort has been made to trace the copyright holders and we apologise in advance for any
unintentional omissions. We would be pleased to insert the appropriate acknowledgement
in any subsequent edition of this publication.

For a complete list of the titles available in the Penguin Active Reading series please write to your local
Pearson Longman office or to: Penguin Readers Marketing Department, Pearson Education,
Edinburgh Gate, Harlow, Essex CM20 2JE, England.

Contents

1.1 What's the book about?

1 Look at the picture on the front of this book. Talk to another student. Do you know anything about the 2005 movie *King Kong*? Did you see it or would you like to see it? What kind of story do you think it is?

2 Which six of these words describe Kong, do you think? Write them next to his picture.

> giant   black   angry   white   strong   gorilla
> short   dangerous   pretty

....

....

....

....

....

....

1.2 What happens first?

On page 1 read the name of Chapter 1 and the sentences in *italics* under it. Then look at the pictures in this chapter. Write answers to these questions. What do you think?

1 How many women are in this story?   ....

2 Does Ann Darrow get a job or a husband?   ....

3 Does Ann think she is in a story about love or hate?   ....

4 Does Jack think she is right?   ....

5 Do you see Jack on page 2 or 8?   ....

A Job for Ann Darrow

"Mr. Denham, I have a question about this love story,"Ann said.
"It's not a love story," Jack said, a little too quickly.

When the Lyric Theater closed its doors for the last time, Ann Darrow had no work and no money. In New York City in 1933, a lot of people were hungry. Ann was hungry, too. She was an **actor** and she had to find a new job quickly.

Carl Denham had work, but his bosses weren't happy with him. They gave him money and he made movies. But when they didn't like a movie, they stopped the money.

With his helper, Preston, Carl showed them the beginning of his new movie and waited.

They didn't like it.

"Where are Bruce Baxter and Maureen McKenzie?" they asked. "Everybody loves them!"

"Maureen wasn't ready," Carl told them angrily. "But I'm changing the story. The actors are coming with me on the ship now."

"What ship?" the bankers asked. "We're not paying for a ship!"

But Carl and Preston were out the door.

"Get the actors and workers on the ship. We're **sailing** tonight," Carl said. He had an old map of a strange **island** and now he wanted to make a very different kind of movie. And he didn't want to wait another day.

A taxi stopped for the two men and they quickly jumped in.

"Carl, Maureen isn't coming. She doesn't want to be in this movie," Preston said.

"Maureen isn't coming?" Carl shouted. "Now I have to find another beautiful woman—and the ship sails in three hours!"

---

actor /ˈæktər/ (n) An *actor* works in the theater or in movies.
sail /seɪl/ (v) A boat or ship *sails* in water from one place to another. *Sailors* work on a ship.
island /ˈaɪlənd/ (n) An *island* is a place in the ocean or a river with water all around it. *Islanders* live on an *island*.

Preston started to ask, "Where's the ship going?" But the taxi stopped and Carl jumped out.

◆

A fruit seller in the street in front of Carl turned his head away from his fruit for a minute and a beautiful young woman quickly took some. But the fruit seller's hand was on her arm before she could run.

"Excuse me," Carl said to the young woman. "I think this fell out of your hand." He gave her money for the fruit. Then he looked at her and smiled. "You're hungry," he said. "Let's go to a restaurant."

In the restaurant Ann told Carl about her life in the theater and Carl told her about his movie.

"The two young people fall in love on the ship," he said. "And then, in the middle of the ocean, they see something ..."

"What?" Ann asked. Now she was interested.

"I don't know," he said slowly. "Jack Driscoll's the writer and he's working on it now."

"Jack Driscoll?" Ann's eyes shone. "He's a wonderful writer. I know his work for the theater, and I love it! I'd like to be in his movie."

When their conversation ended, Carl gave her Maureen McKenzie's job on his new movie.

Later that evening, on the ship, Ann looked out at the lights of New York City and said goodbye to her home.

◆

Jack Driscoll found a table and chair for his dark, dirty room and started to work on the new story. He was on the ship only because Carl was his friend. He didn't want to be there, but you couldn't say no to Carl.

Jack's room was the worst because it usually had animals in it. The ship's boss, Englehorn, and his sailors caught wild animals and sold them for a lot of money. They used **chloroform** because they didn't want to kill the animals. So there were a lot of bottles of chloroform in Jack's room.

Jack wasn't happy about Maureen. Who was this Ann Darrow? Bruce Baxter, the famous movie actor, was unhappy about Ann, too. He only worked with the best actors. But Carl wasn't interested. He had bigger problems. He had to finish this movie and make a lot of money.

In Jack's room, Carl and Jack discussed the story.

"Bruce Baxter is really expensive," Carl told his friend. "And I want us to get rich from this movie!"

chloroform /ˈklɔrəˌfɔrm/ (n) Doctors use *chloroform* when they want people, or animals, to sleep.

3

"Where are we going?" Jack asked. "Tell me—I have to know. I'm writing the story."

"OK, but don't tell *anybody*. The men on this ship won't like it. We're going to **Skull** Island, Jack."

The door opened and Jimmy, the youngest sailor on the ship, came in with some breakfast for the two men. They didn't look up.

"Skull Island…" Jack said quietly. Then he saw Jimmy and stopped talking.

Jimmy's face didn't change. He put down the food and left. The sky was blue and the sun shone every day of the trip.

Ben Hayes, Englehorn's smartest and best sailor, thought, "This trip is starting very well, but I don't like it. Something is going to happen." He looked at his map. Suddenly and angrily, he threw it down. "This isn't the right way," he thought.

Quickly, he went to Englehorn.

Englehorn listened to Hayes. Then he said, "We're going a different way this time."

"But it's dangerous this way," Hayes said angrily. "It's famous for bad weather—you know that!"

"Life on a ship is dangerous," Englehorn answered.

"How much did Denham pay you?" Hayes asked angrily. "Where are we *really* going?"

◆

skull /skʌl/ (n) When somebody falls on his head, he can break his *skull*.

Later that day, Bruce and Ann were in front of the camera. Carl was behind it with Herb, his cameraman, next to him. Jack watched Ann and he liked her work. Bruce was a very good actor, too, but he knew it.

"Mr. Denham, I have a question about this love story," Ann said.

"It's not a love story," Jack said, a little too quickly.

Ann didn't look at him. He was the writer, but she spoke to her boss. She knew him better than Jack Driscoll. She could talk to Carl more easily.

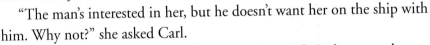

"The man's interested in her, but he doesn't want her on the ship with him. Why not?" she asked Carl.

"He likes her, but … he doesn't want to show it," Carl answered.

She turned to Jack. "Is that right, Mr. Driscoll?" she asked.

"No … OK, yes," Jack said. "He *is* interested. She's very … beautiful and …" He looked for the right words but couldn't find them.

"Yes, she's beautiful, but she's more than that. She's … But maybe I read it wrong," Ann said.

"This is a smart girl with good ideas," Jack thought. "No," he answered quietly. "I think you're right. I wrote it wrong." He thought, "Ann is beautiful, too."

Women were often a problem for Jack. He couldn't find the right words when he was with them. They didn't understand him because he didn't say much. Ann wanted to like him but he was difficult.

Carl shouted, "Preston, I want the other camera from my room. Go and get it."

Preston ran to Carl's room and looked inside a very large box. He couldn't find the camera, but he found an old map of an island with some writing on the back. He tried to read the words. Suddenly, he understood. His mouth and eyes opened wide.

The door opened and Preston quickly put the map under his shirt. Carl walked in.

"Can't you find it? Look, here it is!" he said. He took the camera off the shelf over his bed and left.

Preston stood and thought. "What's happening? Is Carl taking us to this island?" he thought.

After that morning in Jack's room, Jimmy had to tell somebody about Skull Island. He went to Hayes because he was almost a father to Jimmy. Two days later, Hayes saw Carl with a map on the table in the dining-room, so he went in. Jimmy and Preston didn't look up from their breakfast.

Hayes spoke to the cook. "Lumpy, do you think we're on our way to Sumatra?" he asked.

"Of course not. We turned southwest," Lumpy answered.

"Listen, men, I'm not looking for problems," Carl said.

"No, but you're looking for something," Jimmy said quietly.

"Yes, that's right, Jimmy," Carl said. He had to tell them now. "Skull Island. We're going to find it and film it. Then we'll show it to the world."

Lumpy said, "In 1926 Mr. Hayes and I met a man on an island out in the ocean. He almost died on Skull Island. He talked about a great wall, one hundred meters high."

"Why did people build the wall?" asked Carl.

"Kong is the answer," said Hayes.

"That's a crazy old story," said Carl. "There was never *really* a **giant** on the island!"

"That man talked about a giant, angry **gorilla**," Lumpy said. "And the next day we found that man dead with his knife in him."

Preston's face went white. Jimmy's face was white, too.

"You only see giant gorillas in movies," Carl said.

"Take your camera and your men to that island," said Hayes, "and you'll never come back."

◆

Jack couldn't stop thinking about Ann and he wanted to give her something. So he started work on another movie and he wrote it for her.

giant /'dʒaɪənt/ (n/adj) A *giant* animal is a very large animal.
gorilla /gə'rɪlə/ (n) A *gorilla* is a large animal. It has hands and can walk on two legs.

When he finished the first twenty pages, he said, "I would like you to read it."

After she read it, Ann said, "I like it!" She laughed. "It's very funny."

"It's for you," Jack said suddenly.

"Why?" Ann asked. She waited for his answer.

Jack took her in his arms. She didn't push him away.

◆

Preston couldn't sleep at night because he was afraid. One morning he walked across the dining-room to Carl and spoke quietly.

"Carl, we have to talk," Preston said. "Now."

Carl looked up. "What about?" he asked.

"The island, Carl," Preston said angrily.

"You have something and it's mine," Carl said angrily to Preston.

Preston pulled out Carl's map. "Twelve men died, Carl," he said. "On *this* island. It's very dangerous and you're looking for it."

"A crazy man made that map," said Carl.

"Think about Jack, Ann, and Herb! They're your friends."

"Yes, and I pay them!" Carl said angrily.

"You have to tell them!" Preston said.

"Do I?" said Carl. "They'll leave. They'll be afraid."

"Afraid? *I'm* afraid!" said Preston.

Ann heard their conversation, but she didn't understand. Something was wrong—she knew that. "Is this trip going to be dangerous?" she thought.

"You're a good worker, Preston, and one day you'll make good movies," Carl said. "But I have to ask you now: Are you afraid…or are you a moviemaker?"

Preston couldn't take his eyes off Carl's map on the table. He tried to read the small writing, but he couldn't.

"I know it's dangerous. But everybody will be **safe** …" Carl said.

Suddenly, Preston said, "Look! It says *Kong!*" There was a very small picture of a face on the map. Was it a gorilla's face? Preston's angry eyes turned to his boss.

safe /seɪf/ (adj) A *safe* place is not dangerous. When you *save* somebody, you take them out of a dangerous place.

2.1 Were you right?

1 Look back at your answers to Activity 1.2 on page iv. Then answer these questions.

a What is Ann's job? ....

b What is Jack's job? ....

c Does Jack like Ann? ....

d Does Ann like Jack? ....

2 Write about Ann's new boss. Who is he? Where and when does she meet him?

1 His name:

....

2 City:

....

3 Country:

....

4 Year:

....

.2 What more did you learn?

Match the names on the left with the jobs on the right.

1 Carl Denham		a	the camera man
2 Preston		b	boss of the ship
3 Englehorn		c	a moviemaker
4 Bruce Baxter		d	a young sailor
5 Jimmy		e	the cook
6 Ben Hayes		f	Carl's helper
7 Herb		g	a famous movie actor
8 Lumpy		h	an older sailor

3 Language in use

Look at the sentence on the right.
Then finish the sentences below in
the same way. Write the letters, a–e.

> **When** they didn't like a movie,
> they stopped the money.

e   **1** When the Lyric Theater closed its doors for the last time,

◯   **2** When their conversation ended,

◯   **3** Jack couldn't find the right words

◯   **4** When he finished the first twenty pages,

◯   **5** I will know the ending

a   when he was with women.

b   Jack said, "I would like you to read it."

c   Carl gave her Maureen McKenzie's job on his new movie.

d   when I finish reading this book.

e   Ann Darrow had no work and no money.

2.4 What's next?

Read the name of Chapter 2 and the sentences in *italics* under it. Then
look at the pictures in this chapter and the new words at the bottom of
each page. Check (✓) the boxes below. What do you think? Who:

	Englehorn	Carl	Ann	Jack
sails the ship?				
goes to the island?				
screams?				
hears a loud roar?				

Skull Island

*When she stopped screaming, something on the island—maybe
a strange animal—roared loudly.*

"Stop the ship! This is too dangerous," Hayes said to Englehorn.

"We'll get out of here and find better weather," Englehorn said. "How much water is under the ship?" he asked his sailors.

Every man on the ship wanted an answer to that question.

Englehorn and Hayes didn't know this way. Were they near **rocks**? They hoped not.

Suddenly, Jimmy **screamed**, "Wall! There's a wall in front of us! We're going to sail into it!"

Englehorn shouted to Hayes, "Stop the ship!"

Hayes quickly tried to stop it but the front of the ship hit the wall.

"Rocks!" screamed Jimmy.

Englehorn could do nothing now. The ship was in dangerous water and moved wildly up and down. Some sailors fell on the floor. Other men ran and shouted. They had to save their ship! Nobody wanted to die on these rocks.

Suddenly, Carl could see Skull Island, a rocky mountain with very old **ruin**s at the top. Its giant black rocks stood out of the water and they looked dangerous.

---

rock /rɑk/ (n) You can find *rocks* on a beach, under water, and in mountains. They are very hard and heavy. A *rocky* place has a lot of rocks.

scream /skrim/ (v/n) People *scream* when they are very afraid. Their mouths are wide open and the sound is loud.

ruin /ˈruɪn/ (n/v) When very old houses and walls fall, they are *ruins*. When people *ruin* things, the things stop being good.

"Here's the movie camera," said Preston to his boss, ready for a day's work.

The two men left quickly but nobody saw them.

"We're taking in a lot of water!" Hayes shouted suddenly.

The sailors worked quickly, but they didn't have much time. They had to get the water out of the ship.

"Come quick!" Jimmy shouted to Englehorn.

Englehorn and Hayes quickly followed Jimmy up the stairs and looked. Four sailors were in a small boat with Carl, Jack, Preston, Ann, Bruce, Herb, and Mike, the sound man.

"They're going to the island," said Jimmy.

"Do you want me to bring them back?" Hayes asked.

"No. We're leaving here as quickly as we can!" Englehorn said angrily. He never liked Denham, but now he hated him.

On the small beach at Skull Island, Carl was as excited as a little boy, but the other visitors weren't. Ann took Jack's hand and looked up at the old ruins and the large **statues** in the rocks. From high above, the statues' angry faces looked down on them.

statue /'stætʃu/ (n) People cut rocks and wood and make *statues* of people or animals. We often see them in parks.

13

"They don't want visitors here," Jack thought.

Carl, Herb, and Mike got the cameras and lights ready.

"OK, Herb, film the statues. Ann, you're afraid. Bruce, put your arm around her. Ann, look up at these statues and then scream," Carl said.

Ann's eyes opened wide and she screamed loudly and wildly.

When she stopped screaming, something on the island—maybe a strange animal— **roared** loudly.

Hayes and Englehorn heard it. They turned quickly and saw hundreds of birds. The birds flew up into the sky, away from the island.

"What was *that*?" Bruce asked.

Nobody answered.

"Herb, bring the camera! Follow me," said Carl.

They climbed quickly up some stairs in the rocks.

"Where are you going? Is this a good idea?" Bruce asked, afraid.

Two sailors waited in the small boat and the other people followed Carl. Ann was last.

Jack looked back at her and said, "Ann?"

"I want to go back to the ship," she said. She spoke quickly.

But Carl shouted, "Come here, everybody! Look!" He was very happy. This strange place was full of old ruins and statues and it was the only place in the world for Carl's new and best movie. He knew it. "Ann, stand over there. Ready, Herb?" he said.

After Herb stopped filming, everybody followed Carl. They went across a very old bridge and saw the skulls of maybe one or two hundred people on the ground. They climbed up over some more rocks and looked down. There were a lot of very old ruins and some small, old houses.

"Nobody lives here now. It's a ruin," said Carl. "Look, more stairs over there go to that large door in the wall. Wait! Look! There's a little girl down there!"

Slowly and carefully, he walked down to the child. She was very dirty with strange, wild eyes.

roar /rɔr/ (v) Large, angry animals open their mouths wide and *roar* loudly.

"Here's some candy," Carl said.

He took some chocolate from his jacket. But when he tried to give it to her, he felt her teeth in his finger. Then, she ran away.

Suddenly, there were more people, young and old. Slowly they came out from behind rocks. They had strange clothes and wild eyes.

Carl called for everybody with him. They, too, went down and saw the islanders.

"They won't hurt us," said Carl.

Without a sound, Mike, the sound man, fell face down on the ground. There was a very long knife in his back—he was dead.

Ann screamed. Quickly, Jack and Carl turned and looked for the killer.

Suddenly, the wild animal roared again, but this time louder and more angrily. Everybody was afraid. Then, wild men jumped out at them and pulled them with their strong hands. An old woman with long, white hair looked angrily into Ann's eyes. Ann felt cold and afraid.

The sky got darker and a heavy rain began to fall. The islanders shouted angrily in their strange language. A fight began when some men pushed one of the sailors onto the ground. They hit him many times over the head with some wood. He died quickly. More men pushed and kicked Carl.

Some people pulled Ann out of Jack's arms and he tried to get her back. But somebody hit him on the head and he fell. Was he dead, too?

Ann screamed loudly and wildly. Everybody turned, afraid, their eyes on the wall.

Suddenly, the sound of a gun changed everything. The islanders ran away, back to their houses. Englehorn walked over to Carl and pulled him up onto his feet.

"Are you ready now?" he asked angrily. "Can we go?"

3.1 Were you right?

1 Look back at your answers to Activity 2.4. Then match the pictures with the words.

sailor

rocks

camera

roar

2 Now write the same words in these sentences.

a Englehorn sails the ship into the ....

b Carl, Ann, and Jack go to the island with four ....

c Ann screams and then she hears a loud ....

d After Englehorn, Carl, Ann, and Jack hear the animal's roar, Carl asks Herb for his ....

3.2 What more did you learn?

Circle the right word(s) in *italics*.

1 Jimmy screams because the *rocks* / *statues* are dangerous.

2 The sailors have to get *the people* / *water* out of the ship.

3 Englehorn is angry when *Hayes* / *Jimmy* shows him Carl in the little boat.

4 Ann screams for the first time because *Bruce* / *Herb* is filming her.

5 After Ann hears the animal's roar, she wants to go *up the stairs* / *back to the ship*.

6 After they go across the bridge, they find *one or two* / *one or two hundred* skulls.

7 The islanders *help* / *kill* Mike and one of the sailors.

8 The islanders run away when they hear *Carl's* / *Englehorn's* gun.

3 Language in use

Look at the sentences on the right. Then write the sentences below in the same way.

> Carl was **as excited as** a little boy.
> We're leaving here **as quickly as** we can.

1 Bruce was afraid and Ann was afraid.

   Bruce was as afraid as Ann.

2 Herb was excited and Carl was excited.

   ....

3 The little girl was strange and the other islanders were strange.

   ....

4 The islander men shouted angrily and the old woman shouted angrily.

   ....

5 The old islanders cried loudly and the young islanders cried loudly.

   ....

4 What's next?

Read the name of Chapter 3 and the sentences in *italics* below it. Then look at the pictures in this chapter. What do you think is going to happen? Discuss these questions and then make notes about the story.

1 Where is Ann?

2 How does she get there?

3 Who gets on the ship?

4 Who is looking for Ann?

5 What animals do you see?

6 What do you know about these animals?

7 Will more people die? Who?

8 Why is the wall important?

Notes

CHAPTER 3

The Wall

"What's happened to Ann?" he thought wildly.
"Did the islanders get on the ship? Do they have her?"

"The ship is too heavy! Throw tables, boxes, everything into the ocean!" Englehorn shouted.

Everybody was back on the ship now but they couldn't get it off the rocks. Sailors carried things out of Lumpy's kitchen and threw them into the water. Englehorn saw Lumpy's sad eyes but he had to save his men and his ship. The water was higher now, so maybe it was possible. But the ship moved wildly up and down.

It was a black night. Nobody saw the islander when he jumped from the island's highest rocks. Everybody on the ship was too busy. His feet hit the floor of the ship without a sound and he moved quickly.

In her room, Ann didn't want to think about Skull Island or Mike, now dead. In her head she could hear the loud roar of that strange animal in the **jungle**.

"What *was* it?" she thought. Jack wasn't dead—she was happy about that. "He'll be OK," she hoped.

Jack woke up in his room. Slowly, he remembered Skull Island, Mike, and the wild islanders. Then he remembered Ann. When she screamed, something in the jungle roared back. What was it? Ann…he had to find her.

He got up slowly and tried to walk. His head hurt really badly and the ship moved quickly up and down, right and left. But he had to find Ann. When he got to her room, the door was wide open. A lot of her things were on the floor, but there was no Ann. Jack felt sick.

"What's happened to Ann?" he thought wildly. "Did the islanders get on the ship? Do they have her?"

◆

jungle /ˈdʒʌŋɡəl/ (n) *Jungles* are hot, wet places with a lot of trees and wild animals.

Herb and Preston sat in Carl's room, but Carl couldn't sit quietly.

"We got away. We have to be happy about that," Carl said.

"But Mike didn't get away," Preston said sadly.

"Mike worked hard for me and he loved his job. I'm going to finish this movie for Mike! We'll give the money to his family."

"Yes, good. We'll do that," Herb said.

Two sailors came to Carl's door.

"We have to throw your bed, table, and more heavy things into the ocean. Everything goes," they said.

"Take it away, boys," said Carl.

The men carried a lot of things out of Carl's room.

"We got some great film there," Herb said.

"We filmed Skull Island!" Carl answered with a smile. "It was dangerous, but now we can finish filming Ann and Bruce in a safe place."

He looked around his room.

"Something isn't right!" he thought. "Where's my camera?" he shouted. Then he jumped up and ran out.

One of the sailors started to throw Carl's camera into the ocean.

Carl shouted, "No! Not that! Stop!"

He jumped and quickly took the camera from the sailor's hands.

"Throw that camera in the water!" Englehorn shouted at Carl. "No more filming! Men are dead because you want to make a movie!"

"Don't come near me or my camera!" Carl shouted angrily.

Englehorn hit Carl in the face and he fell. The camera flew across the floor. Suddenly, the ocean pushed the front of the ship up high, and Englehorn fell. Carl jumped up and saved his camera.

There was a long, loud noise from the bottom of the ship. And then—away from the rocks—they were free!

◆

Jack ran down some stairs. At the bottom he found a dead man on the floor but he couldn't stop. He had to find Ann before it was too late. He looked around wildly. Which way did they go?

At the same time, Hayes carefully turned the ship around and sailed out into the ocean. The men shouted happily. Now they could go home.

"We're free now," Englehorn thought. "You did that very well," he said to Hayes. Then he turned and saw Jack.

"Stop!" Jack shouted. "We have to turn back! It's Ann! She's not on the ship!"

Englehorn's eyes turned to the island. "Those people have other plans for us," he said.

◆

A lot of water went into Ann's mouth and hurt her eyes. The man had one arm around her and a **rope** in his other hand. Other men stood on the island with the other end of the rope and pulled them out of the water. They had her now.

Ann was very weak and she couldn't scream.

◆

Hayes looked at the men's faces. Every sailor on the ship liked Ann and wanted to get her back safely. He looked at Englehorn.

Englehorn thought carefully for a minute. Then he shouted, "Get ready, men—we're going back!"

They quickly put two small boats into the water and threw guns into them. Carl and Jack helped.

Jack saw fires on the top of the great wall. They shone in the dark night sky and there was a lot of smoke.

"Will they kill her in those fires?" he thought.

The two small boats went out onto the ocean with Carl, Preston, Bruce, Herb, Jack, Englehorn, and twenty sailors. Hayes and Lumpy got another boat ready.

"We don't have much time," Hayes thought.

◆

In the dark, the islanders pushed Ann to the wall. The heavy rain didn't put out the fires on the top of it. Some old people cried, afraid of the

---

rope /rəʊp/ (n) You throw a *rope* to somebody and pull them out of dangerous water.

animal behind the wall. They shouted angrily at Ann in their strange language. They repeated one word many times: *Kong!* But what did it mean?

"The men will come. They'll save me!" Ann thought. But she was very afraid. These wild people were afraid, too—she could see it in their eyes. There was something over that wall and it was very dangerous. They were safe only because the wall was between them and it.

An old woman with wild red eyes stood in front of Ann now. She talked fast and crazily. The men pushed Ann to the ground and the old woman jumped at her. She threw something from a bottle into Ann's face.

Ann understood. "They're going to give me to *that thing* over the wall," she thought. "They'll live and I'll die…for them!"

They took her to the bridge at the top of the wall and put ropes around her arms and legs.

Ann tried to get free of the ropes but she couldn't. Men brought more fire, and for the first time she could see below her. Across a wide **ravine** at the bottom of the wall, there was a bed of rocks. The dark jungle behind it looked very dangerous.

The islanders cried and screamed loudly.

Suddenly, the ropes moved and Ann went down into the ravine.

On the bed of rocks, Ann saw fire all around her. She could see faces of statues in the hot light of the fire. Was this their theater and was she the actor? Then there was smoke all around her and she couldn't see. She felt very weak and everything hurt.

The islanders stopped shouting.

ravine /rə'vin/ (n) A *ravine* is an opening between two high mountains.

Through the smoke Ann saw something very big and dark. It jumped quickly through the trees on its heavy feet. Ann's eyes and mouth opened wide, but she couldn't scream.

Suddenly, she saw it—a giant gorilla, about eight meters tall! She couldn't take her eyes off his ugly black face. He was an intelligent animal—she could see that in his eyes. On his face were old cuts from many fights.

Suddenly, he roared louder than before.

Ann screamed. The islanders up above her on the wall cried and screamed, too.

Kong put out his large black hand and easily pulled Ann from the ropes. He carried her away into the thick jungle.

Then she heard guns.

"Too late. You're too late!" she cried.

◆

Englehorn and the sailors shot into the sky and the islanders ran into the ruins. Some ran to their houses. When Jack was almost to the wall, he heard Ann's screams. Then he heard the loud, angry roar of an animal.

"What was that?" Englehorn asked.

Jack couldn't answer. He climbed up the stairs next to the wall. He looked down at Carl. Carl's eye was at a small opening in the wall. When he moved back, his face was white.

"What is it?" Jack shouted. "What can you see?"

Carl didn't answer.

At the top, Jack looked down. He could see the rocks and statues below, and the nearest trees were on fire.

"I can't see her!" he shouted to the other men.

Carl knew. A giant gorilla, something from another world, had Ann.

"I would really like to film that giant," he thought. "Is it possible? Yes, I can do it and I'll be famous!"

It was a dangerous plan, but he had to do it.

Hayes arrived on the island with more sailors and more guns. He walked over to Carl and looked at him angrily.

"What did you see, Denham?" Hayes asked. "What kind of animal is it?"

"I don't know," he said. "I think it was a kind of gorilla."

Jack tried to break open a door at the bottom of the wall. He couldn't do it, so Hayes shot it open with his gun.

Then he gave Jack a gun. But when Hayes saw Jimmy with a gun in his hands, he took it away.

"Not you, Jimmy," Hayes said.

"I want to help! I'm a man, not a boy!" Jimmy said to Hayes.

"You're staying here," Hayes answered.

Carl, Herb, and Preston had the cameras and film for this trip into the jungle. Englehorn watched them angrily, but he said nothing.

"I'm going to save Miss Darrow … *and* my job," Carl told him.

Bruce Baxter also had a gun—but for the first time it wasn't for a movie. Hayes and ten sailors were ready, but Englehorn and the other men stayed behind.

"You have guns and food and twenty-four hours," Englehorn said. "At this time tomorrow, we're sailing out of here."

Jack pushed through the open door and the other men followed. The night was dark and strange noises came from the jungle. Suddenly, the men heard a very loud noise and everything moved. Was it an animal? They shot at it, but they couldn't see it. It fell noisily at their feet—dead.

"It's a **dinosaur!**" shouted one of the sailors.

Carl quickly took his camera from Herb. But before he could do anything, there was another dinosaur in front of them.

They tried to kill the dinosaur but it ran at them.

Hayes shot it between the eyes and it fell to the ground.

Kong ran with Ann in his hand up to the top of some rocks. When he sat down, he looked at her face carefully…and she looked at his.

Kong turned her—head down and feet up—and below her she saw the skulls of many dead people! She screamed.

Then she heard a shot a long way away.

"Jack!" she screamed. "I hope he finds me," she thought.

Later on that dark night, Jack and the other men arrived at the same place, but Ann wasn't there. They saw the skulls and were afraid for her.

Hayes turned his head and saw one of the sailors with his hat down over his face. He pulled the hat off. It was Jimmy, with a gun in his hands.

"What are you doing here?" Hayes asked. "You're too young."

"I want to help," Jimmy said. "I want to find Miss Darrow."

Hayes turned away. "Come, let's go!" he shouted to his men.

dinosaur /ˈdaɪnəˌsɔːr/ (n) *Dinosaurs* were very large animals and they lived before man.

Five hours later, the morning sun was hot and they were very tired. They had to stop and put down their heavy guns.

Carl didn't want to lose a minute. He had to film Bruce.

He said, "Come here, Bruce. Ready, Herb?"

"Why don't we wait…for Ann?" Preston said.

"Look at this place!" Herb said. "It's as good as money in the bank. This movie isn't about her now!"

A very loud noise came out from behind some trees. The men's eyes opened wide and then about one hundred dinosaurs ran at them.

Hayes screamed, "Run!"

More dinosaurs ran down from some high rocks. The men ran for their lives, but the dinosaurs were very fast. Two men died under their feet. Bruce turned and shot one dinosaur. It fell heavily and then other dinosaurs fell on top of it. Carl and Jack fell, too.

Jack quickly climbed out from under a dinosaur and ran.

"Go!" Hayes shouted to Jack. Then he killed two more dinosaurs.

"Where's Carl?" Jack shouted. "Carl! Carl!"

Carl climbed out from under a dinosaur with his camera in his arms. The two men ran as fast as their legs could go. Hayes killed more dinosaurs, and then he followed them.

The men quickly climbed up some very high rocks, but the dinosaurs were right behind them. One of the sailors fell. A dinosaur caught him in its big teeth. The man screamed.

With his camera in one hand, Carl put out his other hand to Herb.

"Herb! Quickly!" he shouted. "Take my hand!"

Herb put out his hand. But his leg turned suddenly and he fell. Three or four dinosaurs quickly caught him in their teeth and ate him.

Carl felt weak and sick. His eyes and mouth opened wide, but he couldn't scream.

"Carl, come!" shouted one of the men above him.

4.1 Were you right?

Look back at your answers to Activity 3.4. Then look at these sentences. Are they right (✓) or wrong (✗)?

1 One of the islanders jumps onto the ship and takes Ann.

2 Ann swims to the island.

3 Englehorn goes back to the island happily.

4 The islanders push Ann to the wall.

5 The islanders take Ann to the bridge at the top of the wall and put ropes on her.

6 The islanders put Ann down into a ravine on a bed of rocks.

7 Ann sees a giant gorilla—eighty meters tall!

8 Dinosaurs kill three sailors, Herb, and Bruce.

4.2 What more did you learn?

Answer these questions.

1 Why does Englehorn want to throw Carl's camera into the ocean?
....

2 Why does Jack want Englehorn to turn back to the island?
....

3 Why do the islanders give Ann to Kong?
....

4 What does Kong do with Ann in Chapter 3?
....

5 What does Carl think when he sees Kong?
....

Language in use

Look at the sentence on the right.
Which sentence in B follows each sentence
in A? Make longer sentences with *so.*

> He couldn't do it, **so** Hayes
> shot it open with his gun.

A	B
1 The ship was too heavy.	**a** The men ran for their lives.
2 Ann wasn't on the ship.	**b** He pulled her out of the ropes.
3 Kong wanted Ann.	**c** The sailors threw things into the ocean.
4 The hungry dinosaurs ran quickly.	**d** Carl couldn't save him.
5 Herb fell suddenly.	**e** Englehorn sailed back.

1 The ship was too heavy, so the sailors threw things into the ocean.

2 ....

3 ....

4 ....

5 ....

.4 What's next?

Look at the pictures in Chapter 4. What will happen? Write *Yes* or *No.*

1 Ann will run away from Kong and find her way to the ship.   ....

2 Kong will kill dinosaurs and save the men.   ....

3 Two more sailors will die.   ....

4 Jimmy will save Ann from a dinosaur.   ....

5 Preston will throw away Carl's camera.   ....

6 Kong will want to kill the men.   ....

A Past World

Afraid, Ann looked around. "How many dinosaurs are here? With Kong, I'm safe," she thought. So she followed him.

The men followed Hayes to a safe place between some high rocks. There was only Carl, Jack, Preston, Bruce, Hayes, Jimmy, and five or six sailors now. They stopped for five minutes and Lumpy looked angrily at Carl. Jack was angry at Carl, too, now because Carl loved his camera more than his friends.

The ground in front of them was very wet and dangerous.

"How much rope do we have?" Jack asked Hayes.

"Are you crazy, Jack? We can't go across there!" Lumpy shouted.

One of the sailors said, "She's dead and we are, too."

"Let's go back," Bruce said. "We only have nine hours before the ship sails."

"We *have* to find Miss Darrow!" shouted Jimmy.

"She's dead, Jimmy," Bruce said quietly.

Jack heard him and looked angrily into his eyes.

"Herb is dead," Carl said to Preston. "But we have to finish this job…

for him. He wanted this film as much as I did…*do*. The money from it will help his wife and children."

"We'll do it, boss, for Herb…" Preston said. They had to live and work for something. Or die! Preston knew this.

◆

Kong ran through the jungle with Ann in his hand and pushed over trees in his way. Suddenly, an ugly great dinosaur jumped out at Kong and tried to take Ann in its teeth.

She screamed.

Kong roared angrily.

Then another dinosaur tried to get her, but Kong killed it easily with his free hand. He put Ann down when they came to some very old ruins. Then he sat down with his back to her.

Ann's arms, legs, and head hurt. She looked around and saw some stairs. Quietly, she slowly moved across the ground on her stomach.

"Will I get away this time?" she hoped.

Suddenly, she jumped up and ran for the stairs. But before she could get away, Kong's hand hit the ground in front of her. He roared angrily.

She stopped. She could do nothing.

Kong watched her with his dark, sad eyes. Then he turned and walked into the jungle. He climbed over the wall of a ruin. Ann watched him go.

She didn't know the way out of the jungle, but she had to try again.

"He can't see me now. I'm free! But are the men looking for me? I hope they are…" she thought.

◆

"We have to get across that wet ground," Hayes said. "We'll use the wood from these trees and build boats."

The men worked quickly with trees and ropes and after a half hour they were ready.

Jack looked around him at the dead trees in the water. "This really is another world," he thought.

Jack hated this wild island but he couldn't leave without Ann.

Suddenly, the boats hit something under the water.

"What was that?" shouted Lumpy.

Something jumped out of the black water and turned their boats over. The men screamed and fell. A giant fish opened its mouth and hungrily took a sailor with its long teeth. The water went red.

Jack saw, but he couldn't help. There were **vines** around his legs and he couldn't get free. His head went under the water. Then it came up, and went under again.

He heard a shout from Carl, "Don't lose it, Preston. Don't lose the camera!"

Suddenly, Carl shot the fish. Jack got his legs free of the vines and swam with Carl. The other men swam, too. But then the giant fish came up out of the water again. With its large teeth, it took another sailor. He screamed for help, but nobody could do anything for him.

When they were on dry ground, the men stood quietly. They looked sadly at the red water.

Hayes remembered his time in France: one hundred and ninety-one days of fighting, the dead men, his friends. This wasn't very different. He turned away from the water and looked around him.

"Look at the ground," he said to the men. "That giant walked through here."

Suddenly, there was a loud noise and Hayes quickly turned around. A dead dinosaur was on the ground behind him. Smoke came from Jimmy's gun.

"Don't think you're so smart," Hayes said to Jimmy. "You're too young for this."

vine /vaɪn/ (n) Vines climb up trees and walls.

30

Jimmy felt bad. "I know you don't think much of me," he said angrily to Hayes.

Hayes walked away.

"He loves you, Jimmy," Lumpy said. "He doesn't want to lose you. Don't be angry."

Jimmy wanted to be a man. He wanted Hayes to understand that. But now he understood Hayes better and he felt happier.

◆

Ann, now free from Kong, tried to find the way back to the ship. She saw smoke about six kilometers away.

"This is the right way back," she thought.

Tired and dirty, she wanted to sit down, but she had to listen carefully. There were more dinosaurs, but where?

Suddenly, there was a noise from behind her and she turned around.

"Is it Jack?" she hoped.

Two large, angry dinosaurs ran at her. Quickly, she jumped under an old tree. She pulled her legs under her so the dinosaurs couldn't get her with their big teeth. Two more dinosaurs came from behind and the four dinosaurs fought angrily.

Ann jumped out and ran.

But another, larger dinosaur came after her with a hungry look in its eyes. The dinosaur's mouth, with its big teeth, came nearer.

Ann screamed.

Before its teeth closed around her, she saw Kong's face behind the dinosaur. His great heavy hand broke the dinosaur's skull. Another dinosaur ran at them but Kong killed it, too.

Ann watched Kong and she felt happy and sad at the same time.

"He saved me," she thought. "But will he take me back into the jungle, away from the smoke, away from the ship?"

But when he finished, Kong didn't **pick** Ann **up**. He turned and walked away.

Afraid, Ann looked around. "How many dinosaurs are here? With Kong, I'm safe," she thought. So she followed him.

pick up /ˌpɪk ˈʌp/ (v) When you *pick* something *up*, you take it off the floor with your hand.

32

He stopped and turned. He looked at Ann's face. Then he walked away again, but more slowly. Ann followed him, but suddenly the sound of guns stopped her.

Angrily, Kong turned to the sound.

He picked Ann up in his large hand and put her on the top of a very high rock. She couldn't get down and run away. Then Kong turned around and ran through the jungle to the sound of the guns—to the men.

Ann couldn't stop him and she couldn't help her friends. The ground moved under Kong's heavy feet and she could hear him roar. Now, she could only wait for Kong.

"Please don't kill them," she thought.

5.1 Were you right?

Look back at your answers to Activity 4.4. Then finish the sentences.

1 Ann runs away from Kong, but then she ....
2 Kong kills dinosaurs and saves ....
3 Two more sailors die in the ....
4 Jimmy shoots a dinosaur and saves ....
5 Preston ....
6 Kong wants to kill the men, so he puts ....

5.2 What more did you learn?

Check (✓) the right picture.

1 Who wants to save Ann?

2 Who is angry at Carl?

3 Who shoots, but doesn't kill, a giant fish?

4 Who does Hayes feel love for?

5 Who feels safe with Kong?

Language in use

Look at the sentence on the right. Then make these words into sentences, with *before* in the right place.

> **Before** she could get away, Kong's hand hit the ground in front of her.

1 the dinosaur could take Ann / Kong killed it

   Before the dinosaur could take Ann, Kong killed it

2 the men could go across the water / they built boats

3 the giant fish ate the sailor / Jack could save him

4 Jimmy killed the dinosaur /Hayes saw it

5 Kong put Ann on a very high rock / he ran through the jungle to the men

What's next?

Look at the pictures in Chapter 5. What is happening? Write a sentence about each picture.

1

2

3

4

Kong Saves Ann

"To this beautiful woman, I am an ugly giant."
He looked at his hands and then, with sad eyes, at Ann.

The men followed Hayes to a giant ravine, thick with trees and vines. One very long dead tree went across it at the top. It was their only bridge.

"OK, men, follow me!" Hayes said. "Jimmy, stay right behind me." The dead tree was wet and dangerous. "Don't look down," he said.

Very carefully, Carl carried his camera across the ravine.

"Maybe now he'll lose that stupid camera," Hayes hoped.

At the other end of their bridge, there were dark ruins and trees with thick, heavy vines. Hayes heard something. He stopped.

Somebody, or something, was there—he could feel its eyes on him.

"What is it?" Jimmy asked quietly.

"Jimmy, maybe you'll have to turn around and run," said Hayes.

"I'm not afraid," answered Jimmy.

"I don't want you to die here, Jimmy," said Hayes. "What's in those ruins?" he thought.

Two angry, yellow eyes shone out of the dark ruins at him.

"Go back!" Hayes shouted to the men behind him.

They turned around quickly. Hayes shot into the ruins. Suddenly, the watcher jumped out at him.

For the first time, Jack saw the giant gorilla. It was as tall as the trees and it ran at Hayes. Its large hand picked him up. Jack's face went white.

Jimmy couldn't leave Hayes. He wanted to help his friend.

"No, Jimmy! Go back!" Hayes shouted.

Hayes was unafraid and he shot Kong in the face. Kong roared angrily. Jimmy and Jack, half the way across the bridge, turned and looked.

Suddenly, Kong threw Hayes across the ravine. The men heard the sound when Hayes hit the north wall of the ravine hard. There was no question—he was dead.

"No!" Jimmy cried.

Kong roared. Jimmy's eyes were wet and very angry. He started to go for Kong—he wanted to kill him. Jack pulled Jimmy down onto the tree.

Suddenly, Kong hit the tree with his heavy hand and Jack and Jimmy fell. Quickly, they put out their hands and caught the vines on the tree. The vines stopped their fall, but it was a long way down to the bottom of the ravine.

"We can't stay here, but we can't move," Jack thought wildly.

Lumpy was almost safely across the bridge. Carl, too, was almost to the other end when he fell onto his stomach. His camera flew out of his hands and into the tree near Lumpy.

"Get it, Lumpy!" he shouted.

But Lumpy kicked the camera and it fell into the ravine.

Suddenly, Kong picked up the dead tree. Carl saw Jack and Jimmy with the vine in their hands, but he couldn't help them. The sailors on the tree tried not to fall, but then two men screamed. When they hit the bottom of the ravine, their skulls broke on the rocks. Then another man screamed and fell.

Kong roared angrily and threw the tree into the ravine. Jack, Jimmy, Carl, and Lumpy went down with it. They fell into some thick, wet, brown water. It was strangely cold. The men were hurt but not badly. Three sailors were dead—Lumpy's best friend was one of them.

Kong turned and walked away.

Jack looked for Jimmy and found him in some vines. He put his arms around the young man and Jimmy cried.

Carl sat up and saw his camera on the rocks. He couldn't use it now. There was black film everywhere.

Suddenly, some ugly underground animals climbed onto Lumpy's dead friend. Before Lumpy could move his friend away, a hundred or more of these strange, ugly animals came up out of the ground.

Jack and Jimmy tried to kill some of them, but there were too many.

Lumpy screamed loudly. One of the animals had his head in its mouth—and then it ate him. More animals arrived before the loud sound of guns came from above.

Bruce Baxter and Preston shot and killed a lot of the ugly things. The other animals ran away.

Suddenly, there were more sailors above them with guns, and with them was Englehorn.

Preston shouted, "Take the rope! I'll pull you up!"

Jack helped Jimmy up and then he went for Carl. He put the end of the rope in Carl's hands. Carl didn't look at him. He had a strange smile on his face.

Englehorn pulled on the rope and helped Carl to the top of the ravine. Then he looked around him.

"What did you do to my men?" he said angrily to Carl. "Why aren't you dead, too?"

He saw Jack, across the ravine. Jack climbed to the top and walked away through the trees.

"Stop! Driscoll! Don't be stupid!" Englehorn shouted.

"I'll see you later," shouted Jack.

"She's dead," Englehorn shouted to him.

Carl stood next to Englehorn and watched Jack.

"She's not dead. Jack's going to bring her back to the ship," he said.

Englehorn looked at Carl. Carl had a new plan, but what was it?

"That gorilla will be right behind Jack, too," Carl said slowly. "We can win this game."

"Are you planning to catch that gorilla and take it home?" Englehorn asked. He laughed at Carl's stupid idea.

"You catch wild animals. And you have a lot of chloroform on the ship. We can use that," Carl said.

"I don't think we can," answered Englehorn.

"Jack, be careful!" Carl shouted to his old friend.

"Don't close the door in the wall!" Jack shouted back.

"I won't!" shouted Carl. After a minute, when Jack couldn't hear, he said quietly, "I'm sorry, Jack."

◆

Kong went back to Ann and took her down from the high rock. For the first time in this jungle, she felt strangely safe. He jumped across a ravine and then across a river. She was a small plaything between his large fingers.

Then he stopped and put her down. She looked up and high above her head was a statue of a giant gorilla.

"That's you, Kong!" she said.

Kong looked at Ann, a very small person, and at the giant statue. He understood something for the first time: "To this beautiful woman, I am an ugly giant." He looked at his hands and then, with sad eyes, at Ann. Slowly and carefully, he picked her up again and took her to a very high mountain. From up there Ann could see the ship, only about five kilometres away.

The orange sun slowly went down in the west. When Kong put Ann down, she saw the skull of a giant gorilla on the ground near her. Was this

his mother's or his father's skull? Maybe his brother's or his wife's? Ann understood. He had nobody and she was his only family now.

Ann put her hand on Kong's arm but he didn't look at her. She wanted to make him happy, so she danced for him. But he didn't look.

"Look at me," she said. "Look!"

Slowly, he turned and put one finger in front of her. She put her arms around it and he pulled her up. She looked across the jungle to the ocean. His eyes followed hers.

"It's beautiful," she said. Kong looked into her pretty face. "Beau-ti-ful!" she repeated slowly.

He opened up his hand and she climbed into it. With one large finger, he slowly felt her hair. She looked into his eyes and she wasn't afraid.

The light of day slowly changed to the dark of night on this mountain top and the two of them sat quietly.

Jack climbed carefully up the dangerous rocks to the top.

When he got there, his eyes opened wide. There was Kong, asleep.

But where was Ann? Slowly, Jack moved nearer to the giant animal. Up above, giant birds flew around and around in the night sky.

Jack was near Kong's feet when he looked up at the gorilla's hand. His eyes opened wider than before. Ann was asleep in Kong's hand!

He moved very slowly, and suddenly, Ann's eyes opened. She was excited, but she didn't make a sound. Jack very slowly walked nearer.

More birds flew above them. Kong moved a little at the noise, but didn't wake up. Jack quickly put out his hand to Ann and she felt his fingers with hers. Then suddenly, Kong's eyes opened and his fingers closed around Ann. He jumped to his feet and roared at Jack.

"Run, Jack!" Ann screamed.

Kong's great hand came down above Jack's head, but Jack jumped away very quickly. Kong put Ann down and turned to Jack. He roared and ran at him. Jack fell to the ground and moved to the right and to the left. Kong's large foot came down, but Jack was too fast for the gorilla.

Suddenly, Ann screamed wildly and Kong turned to her. Jack ran to a safer place behind a tree, but he could see giant birds around Ann's head. The birds tried to take her off of the rock, but she fought back. Kong ran and roared angrily at the birds. He picked Ann up and fought the birds with his free hand. But now there were too many of them and he had to put her down. The birds fought hard and were very strong. There were cuts on Kong's large arms, but he didn't stop. He had to save Ann.

Jack quickly ran and took Ann's hand. There was only one way out of there. It was almost two thousand meters to the bottom of the mountain, but they had to try. Ann put her arms around Jack and he caught a thick vine in his hands. With Ann on his back, he jumped. Hand over hand, he climbed down the vine.

Kong roared from above. Jack looked up and saw the gorilla with two giant birds on his back. Kong quickly pulled them off and killed them. The other birds flew away.

"No! Don't go! We have to have a little more time," Jack thought.

Jack and Ann were only one hundred meters down the vine when Kong began to pull them up. A giant bird came back and flew around them. Jack took one hand off the vine and caught the bird's foot.

Then Jack quickly took his other hand off the vine and took the bird's foot. But he and Ann were too heavy, so the bird started to fall. Jack looked down and below them he saw a fast river. His hands left the bird's feet and they fell.

Ann screamed.

Above them, Kong roared.

The river carried Jack and Ann away very quickly, but after a minute or two they came to a quieter, slower place in the river. They swam out and fell on the ground. They were very weak, but they weren't dead.

"Jack?" Ann said.

"Here I am," he answered.

"Did he follow us?"

"He will."

Ann turned her head and looked at Jack. She was wet, dirty, and very afraid. But he saw a different Ann.

"She is really beautiful…" he thought. And suddenly, he felt better.

"Thank you," said Ann.

"For what?" he asked her.

"You saved me. Only you," she answered.

He wanted to say something, but he couldn't find the right words. He put out his hand and felt her face. She put her hand out to him. Then he moved away from her. Ann didn't understand, so she pulled away, too.

Before Jack could say anything, Kong roared above them. They quickly jumped up and looked up at the mountain top. Kong's heavy feet came nearer, so they ran for their lives.

Ann felt very bad about Kong now. "I'm his only family and he saved me," she thought. "But I want to go home!" She was afraid and felt sad for Kong at the same time.

Ann and Jack ran very fast through the jungle, and the trees and vines cut their faces and arms. Suddenly, in front of them, they saw…the wall! There was the rock bed at the bottom of the great wall.

Kong roared and roared, louder and angrier. Between the wall and the rock bed was the ravine. There was the bridge—Ann remembered it well. But it was up and they couldn't go across.

"Put down the bridge!" Jack screamed.

"Help us! Please!" Ann cried. She turned.

Kong broke down the last trees between them and him.

Ann looked up at the wall and said, "They left. They're not here."

"Carl!" Jack shouted.

◆

The morning sky was a beautiful color. Behind the wall, Carl heard his friends. But he did nothing. Preston, Jimmy, Bruce, and Englehorn stood behind him.

"Put the bridge down!" Preston said angrily to his boss.

"Wait…" Carl answered.

One of the sailors had a big knife in his hand. He was ready, but he waited for Carl's word. Carl said nothing.

Preston said angrily, "No. You're not the boss now."

He quickly took the knife from the sailor and cut the rope. It flew back at him and cut his face badly. The bridge went down and Carl saw Kong's eyes behind Jack.

With the bridge down, Jack and Ann ran across it. At the same time, Kong jumped over the ravine. Jack and Ann ran through the open door in the wall. Then they stopped and looked back.

Two sailors had **chains** in their hands and were ready. Preston was near and he, too, was ready. He tried to clean his cut face with his shirt. The shirt turned dark red, but he didn't have time for that now. Englehorn was ready, too, with a large bottle of chloroform.

"What are you doing?" Ann asked Englehorn.

Kong roared angrily and tried to break down the wall. He found a small weak place and kicked it hard many times.

chain /tʃeɪn/ (n) You put *chains* on a bike so nobody takes it.

"Get ready!" Englehorn shouted.

Kong angrily broke through the wall and ran. But then he stopped and looked around. His eyes found Ann.

Then Kong put out his hand to her.

"Do it now, Englehorn!" shouted Carl.

Englehorn turned to his men and said, "Now!"

The sailors jumped up and ran at Kong with their ropes and chains. Jack watched angrily. But what could he do?

"No!" Ann cried.

"Carl, are you crazy?" Jack shouted.

Some sailors on the wall were ready, too. When Englehorn shouted to them, they threw a large bag down on top of Kong. Then they quickly put chains on him. He was on the ground, but he didn't stop fighting.

"Chloroform!" Carl shouted to Englehorn.

Ann cried, "No, don't do this!"

She started to run to Kong, but Jack took her arm.

"Ann, he'll kill you!" Jack said.

"No, he won't," she cried. She had to help him.

When Kong tried to get up, Englehorn threw the bottle of chloroform into Kong's mouth and eyes. Then the men pushed giant rocks off the top of the wall onto Kong's head.

Ann ran from Jack's arms to Englehorn and caught his arm.

"Stop it! You're going to kill him!" she shouted.

Englehorn looked at Jack and shouted, "Take her away!"

Jack wanted to save Kong, but first he had to save Ann. He pulled her to the beach, away from the men, away from the gorilla.

Suddenly, Kong stood up and roared loudly.

"We can't stop him!" shouted one of the sailors.

"Kill it!" shouted Englehorn. "Shoot it!"

"No! I want him…but not dead!" Carl shouted.

But Kong was free of the ropes and chains and ran for Ann.

"Get in the boat," Jack said to Ann.

Sailors from the ship were there in the two small boats.

"No! He wants me. I can stop this!" Ann shouted.

Kong roared angrily from above and Jack pushed Ann into the boat.

"Take her," he said.

"Take your hands off me! I'm going to him," she shouted angrily.

Englehorn jumped into the little boat with Ann and Bruce.

"Let's get away from here now!" he shouted.

Jack and Jimmy got into a second boat with Carl and Preston. Jimmy wanted to shoot Kong, but Carl stopped him. Ann watched Carl's hands when he opened another bottle of chloroform. She felt very sad and angry, but she couldn't do anything.

Jimmy shot Kong in the leg. Now Kong was angrier and more dangerous. He quickly ran to the boat and hit it hard. Carl fell into the water, with the bottle of chloroform in his hand. Kong picked the boat up out of the water. Sailors screamed and fell into the ocean. Kong picked up the boat and threw it onto some rocks.

Jack came up from under the water with Jimmy under one arm. Kong looked at Ann.

"Go back!" she shouted to him.

Englehorn shot Kong in the leg and he fell. Ann cried and tried to get out of the boat. One of the men stopped her. Carl was on some rocks and Kong was near him now. Carl opened the bottle of chloroform and threw it in Kong's face.

Kong's eyes closed and he put out his hand to Ann. Then he fell onto his back, asleep.

Ann felt cold. She thought, "Kong's life is changing here on this beach. It'll never be the same again."

But Carl stood next to Kong and smiled happily. He shouted, "The world will see him! We're rich! His name will be in lights on Broadway*: Kong, the Giant Gorilla from a Past World!"

---

*Broadway: New York City's theater center

6.1 Were you right?

Look again at the pictures in Chapter 5 and choose the right answer.

1 What is Hayes saying?

    a "I don't want you to die here."

    b "Shoot that animal!"

2 How does Jimmy feel? Why?

    a He is happy because Jack isn't dead.

    b He is sad because Hayes is dead.

3 Where is Kong? What is Kong doing?

    a Kong is sleeping on the mountain top.

    b Kong is jumping across the ravine.

4 Where are Ann and Jack? What do they see?

    a They are next to the river and see Kong.

    b They are across the bridge and see sailors with chains.

6.2 What more did you learn?

What happens at the ravine? Put the numbers of the sentences under the right pictures.

1 He throws Hayes across the ravine.

2 Strange animals eat him and his friend.

3 He pulls Carl out of the ravine.

4 He kills three sailors.

5 He kicks Carl's camera into the ravine.

6 He arrives with more sailors and more guns.

.3 Language in use

Look at the sentence on the right.
Then finish each sentence with *too* and
one of these words.

> Kong's large foot came
> down, but Jack was **too
> fast** for the gorilla.

| difficult | strong | slow | weak | heavy |

1 The giant birds tried to kill Kong, but he was ....
   for them.

2 Jack and Ann were .... for the bird, so it couldn't
   stay up.

3 Jack wanted to say something to Ann, but it was
   .... for him.

4 Ann and Jack shouted to Carl, but he was .... ,
   so Preston cut the rope and the bridge went down.

5 Kong was .... after Carl threw the chloroform into
   his face. He couldn't try to get Ann after that.

6.4 What's next?

Read the name of Chapter 6 and the sentences in *italics*. Look at the
pictures in this chapter. What happens to these by the end of the story,
do you think? Make notes.

Carl	
Jack	
Ann	
Bruce	
Kong	

Kong in New York City

Suddenly, Kong broke free from his chains. People started to understand. Nobody was safe. They screamed.

I n New York's Times Square, Preston stood across the street from the Alhambra Theater and looked up at the lights above its doors. "KONG, GIANT FROM A PAST WORLD," he read.

People got out of taxis and a long line of people waited outside the theater in the snow. There were no more tickets, but they wanted to go in.

Preston felt unhappy about Carl's money-making plan for Kong and he didn't really want to see it. But after tonight he could leave Carl and forget about Skull Island. He wanted to sleep well again at night.

Ann sat in her little dressing room in the back of the theater. She was almost ready. She didn't feel happy in the theater now, but she had to work. After those two days on Skull Island, everything about her life felt strange.

Preston sat down inside the theater and looked around for Carl. He saw him up front with the bankers. They looked happy. But when Carl saw Preston, he quickly turned his head. Then he smiled for a newspaperman with a camera.

Jack Driscoll was in another theater on 42nd Street. He sat and watched the actors in his new story. But he couldn't stop thinking about Ann. Kong was in the Alhambra Theater that same night—he knew that.

"Is Ann there, too?" he thought—he hoped. He left the theater and walked quickly to Times Square. He had to see her.

◆

Carl was as excited as the people in the theater.

"Thank you! Thank you!" he said to them. "I'm going to tell you a very strange story. On a dangerous trip to Skull Island with my actors, seventeen people lost their lives. They died when they tried to save a young woman from a giant animal. You'll see this giant here tonight. He saw a beautiful young woman from New York and he loved her. You all know stories about an ugly animal's love for a beautiful woman …"

◆

In her dressing room, Ann looked beautiful in her long, white dress. Her yellow hair shone under the lights. But she was a different person now and nothing could change that.

"Are you ready, Miss Darrow?" a man at her door asked.

"Wait a minute…" said Ann.

◆

"Here he is! Kong!" shouted the happy Mr. Denham.

The people jumped when they saw Kong. Some almost screamed. Jack stood in the back of the theater and he understood. He remembered the first time for him, too.

Kong sat on the floor with his hands and legs in heavy chains. Jack felt a little sad for him. Then some men pulled on the chains from above and pulled Kong to his feet. Again, some people almost screamed.

"Now you will meet Mr. Bruce Baxter!" Carl said. "Mr. Baxter saved the young woman from this dangerous giant!"

The people loved the famous actor and shouted his name loudly. Then Carl told them about the wild islanders. When he finished, girls in strange clothes came out and danced in front of Kong. The giant gorilla wasn't interested.

Jack watched the dancers, but he didn't like them.

A man next to him said, "We learned something about Carl on that trip. When he loves something, he ruins it."

Jack turned his head and saw Preston. He was right.

"Now you can meet our beautiful young woman!" Carl shouted happily. "Miss Ann Darrow!"

Jack felt sick. "How can she do this?" he thought. He remembered the trip back to New York when she didn't speak to anybody.

A woman in a long white dress came out and stood on a bed of rocks in front of Kong. The gorilla looked carefully at her.

"This is strange," Jack thought. "Doesn't he remember Ann?"

Then Kong's eyes opened wide and shone angrily at this strange woman. He roared and roared.

Jack understood. "That's not Ann!" He turned to Preston and said, "Where is she?"

◆

In another theater Ann danced with other girls in long, white dresses. She tried hard on this night not to think about Skull Island. But she couldn't stop thinking about Jack.

"He loved me, I know that. But he couldn't tell me. Why? Something wasn't right between us ... but what?"

◆

Jack asked again, "Where is she?"

"I have no idea," answered Preston. "Carl wanted her to do this, but she said no. So he found another girl."

Men from the newspapers took a lot of photos of the woman and the gorilla. Kong didn't like the lights from the cameras and he roared angrily.

"Come, Denham," shouted one of these men. "We want a photo of you with the gorilla."

Carl pulled Baxter into the photo with him. "Here's your story, boys," he said. "This man saved the beautiful woman from the dangerous giant gorilla, the great Kong!"

Kong pulled harder and more angrily at his chains and roared wildly. Preston looked at Jack and they felt afraid.

"We have to get these people out of here!" Jack said. "He's going to break the chains!"

"You have to leave," Preston said to a man in front of him.

"Everybody has to leave!" Jack said more loudly.

"Do you know that I paid $10 for these tickets?" the man said.

Suddenly, the woman in the long white dress screamed. One of Kong's hands was free. People saw but they didn't understand. Some people laughed and other people shouted happily.

"Get out of here now!" shouted Jack to the people around him. "Go!"

Again, Kong roared angrily and very loudly. Jack saw Carl's face—a child's face with wide open eyes, but not afraid. Suddenly, Kong broke free from his chains.

People started to understand. Nobody was safe. They screamed. Everybody jumped up and ran for the doors. The woman in white screamed, too. Kong picked her up and threw her across the room.

Jack wanted to help people, but he felt afraid, too. Kong moved through the people and killed many of them with his feet. He stopped

when he saw Jack. Jack saw Kong's angry eyes and he jumped out of his way. Kong tried to find him, and killed more people under his feet.

Jack ran down some stairs and out the door. He ran into the center of Times Square and looked back at the theater.

Suddenly, Kong pushed the walls down and jumped into the street. He looked around at the cars, the lights, and the people.

But Kong didn't see Jack. He was angry and afraid in this strange world of lights and noise. He picked up a woman with yellow hair. She screamed.

Jack saw and understood. "He's looking for Ann!"

❖

When Ann walked out of the theater, she heard screams and the sound of police cars from Times Square. She knew—Kong was there. She ran.

❖

Kong picked up more women with yellow hair. When he saw their faces, he threw them down again. He killed people in their cars with his big feet. He picked up a bus and threw it out of his way. Then he walked out of Times Square and went south.

Jack got into a taxi and said, "Follow him."

The man said, "*You* can follow him, not me!"

He got out of his taxi and Jack quickly drove after Kong. But when Kong saw Jack in the taxi behind him, he roared angrily. Jack quickly turned down a small street and drove south. Other cars had to move quickly out of his way.

Kong was behind Jack and moved fast. Suddenly, Jack hit a wall. Kong didn't see Jack under the ruins and ran past him. Then Kong stopped and stood quietly. What did he see in front of him?

"Oh, no," Jack thought. "Not her! But, of course … she's here. She wants to help … him."

Ann ran to Kong. He looked into her eyes and she smiled at him. Kong put out his hand and picked her up slowly and carefully. Then he carried her away into the New York City night.

The police didn't want to catch Kong; they wanted to kill him. They shot at Kong. But with Ann in his hand, he climbed up onto the top of the highest stores and banks and ran.

Suddenly, he stopped. Across 34th Street, he could see the Empire State Building, the tallest in the world.

Below, in the street, Jack thought about Ann and his mistakes. "Why didn't I tell her about my love for her? Now it's too late. It didn't have to end this way. I have to save her ... I have to save our future."

One hundred or more men with guns were ready on the ground. Kong roared angrily down at them.

A policeman shouted, "Shoot!"

Jack felt sick. "It can't end this way," he thought wildly. "Ann will die!"

The men shot at the gorilla, but suddenly Kong jumped across 34th Street to the Empire State Building. Quickly, he put Ann on his back and started to climb up.

Everybody's eyes were on the gorilla.

Jack ran. "I have to save Ann. I'll get into the Empire State Building through that door there," he thought. Nobody could stop him.

Ann looked down hundreds of meters to the ground below and felt afraid. A strong, cold wind pulled at her, but she didn't scream.

Kong climbed higher and higher. When he was almost at the top, he carefully put Ann down.

"Why are we here? Why did Jack have to save me on Skull Island? This is the worst end for everybody," she thought.

She looked sadly at Kong. Kong sat down and looked across New York City.

Ann thought about the mountain top in the jungle. "Does he think we are safe here? Maybe ... but this time he's wrong."

The sun started to come up and the sky was a pretty color. Kong looked at Ann and she understood.

"Yes, it is beautiful," she said.

She looked up and saw four airplanes with large guns. Kong looked, too, and then at Ann. He roared and pushed her to the wall behind him. The airplanes were nearer now.

"No!" she screamed.

The airplanes came at Kong from the north, south, east, and west and shot him. He roared again, and then started to climb higher.

Ann watched him. "He left me here because it's safer for me," she thought. "But it's not safer for *him*! I'll climb up to him. Maybe they won't shoot when they see me next to him."

She started to climb up.

Kong tried to hit one of the airplanes. He tried again and this time he hit it hard. It fell to the ground, but he fell, too. He put his hand through a window and stopped his fall. But he hit the wall hard and Ann fell from the building. Quickly, Kong put out a hand and caught her.

For a minute, Ann felt safe again. The three other airplanes came nearer and Kong put Ann safely inside through the window. The guns got louder and louder. Kong, badly hurt, roared louder, too. He climbed higher.

Suddenly, Jack arrived and saw Ann. She ran to the stairs. The guns didn't stop and he had to jump out of the way.

The airplanes went around and around over Kong's head. Kong, now at the top of the building, put out his hand and caught one of them. He threw it at one of the other airplanes and, with a loud noise, they lit up the night sky with a great ball of fire.

Ann ran up onto the top and stood between Kong's legs. More airplanes with guns came and she screamed, "No! No!"

They shot Kong again and again and he slowly went down on the floor. Ann took one of his fingers and cried.

Kong picked her up and looked at her. Then he looked to the east. A new day slowly began. He put her down and his face changed. Now he was quiet—and free. His life was at an end.

He fell off the building.

Ann looked down and for a minute she wanted to follow Kong. There was no place for her in this cold world.

Suddenly, she felt Jack next to her.

"Ann…" he said quietly.

"Why are you here?" she asked. Her eyes were wet and red.

His face changed. She saw a new Jack, free from his past life.

"Because I love you," he answered quickly.

Ann looked into Jack's eyes and she slowly moved into his arms. They stood, weak and sad, but with new hope, in the morning light.

Two or three hundred people in the street stood around Kong and the newspapermen took photos of him.

One newspaperman looked up. "Why did he do that? Climb up there? He couldn't run away," he said.

"He was a stupid animal," said another newspaperman. "He didn't know anything."

Carl looked up and said, "He knew. He couldn't have her, so he had to die."

1 **It is two days after Kong dies. Work with three other students and have this conversation.**

Student A:	You are Ann. You want the people of New York to understand Kong. Talk on the radio about Kong's life in New York and on Skull Island. Answer questions.
Student B:	You work for the radio station. Ask Ann questions.
Students C and D:	You are listening at home, and you also have questions. Call the radio station when you want to ask one.

2 **Look at the picture below. Discuss these questions with other students.**

1 How was life difficult or dangerous for Ann on Skull Island? How was it difficult or dangerous for her in New York? Are the two places different in every way?

2 How did Ann want the story to end? How did Kong want it to end? Were their hopes possible? Why (not)?

3 Does anybody in the story feel happy at the end? Who? Why?

Write a letter from Carl to Herb's family. Tell them:

- about the trip to Skull Island
- about Herb's love for his work on the movie
- that it was a dangerous job
- that he saw a lot of strange and exciting things
- about the end of his life
- that you are very sorry

December 28, 1933

Dear Mrs. Jones and Family,

Carl Denham

1 **Why do people like the story of *King Kong*? Work with other students and write notes.**

....

....

....

....

....

....

....

2 **Read about the famous moviemaker from New Zealand, Peter Jackson. Why did he make *King Kong* (2005)?**

Use the Internet and learn more about him. Then work with one or two other students and think about a conversation between Peter Jackson and his bankers. When Jackson asked them for $200,000,000, what questions did the bankers ask Jackson? What were his answers? What do you think? Have the conversation.

When Peter Jackson was nine years old, he saw the movie *King Kong* (1933) on TV. He loved the movie and that giant gorilla. He cried when Kong fell off the Empire State Building. Jackson got his first movie camera when he was eight years old. He had a lot of good ideas for his short movies and he used light and sound in exciting ways. He thought, "I want to make a new King Kong movie some day." So in 1996 he started writing his movie. Jackson is now as famous as his old friend King Kong.

Do you know these famous men?

Which is Steven Spielberg? Alfred Hitchcock? Stanley Kubrick? George Lucas? What movies did they make? Find answers on the Internet. Discuss their movies and the actors in them. Then write about one of the men below.

I like .... because ....

....

....

....

....

....

....

....

....

....

....

....

4 **Work with other students.**

a There are other movies with the same story of an ugly man or animal and a beautiful woman. Can you name some?

b Plan a movie with this story. Where will it happen and when? Who are the animal or the man and the woman? How will the movie end?

Notes

c Write about your movie for a newspaper.

- What is the name of the movie?
- Who are the most important actors?
- When and where can people see the movie?
- In one or two sentences, what is the story about?

....

....

....

....

....

....

....

....

....

....

....

....

....